HORSE PRINCESS

Story by

Maria Iskander

HORSE PRINCESS
Copyright © Maria Iskander
First published 2025

ISBN: 978-1-7638032-1-3

All rights reserved. Without limiting the rights under copyright reserved above, no part of this publication may be reproduced, stored in or introduced into a database and retrieval system or transmitted in any form or by any means (electronic, mechanical, photocopying, recording or otherwise) without the prior written permission of the owner of the copyright.

Original illustrations/ Photographs by: Cecilia

Published with the assistance of Angel Key Publications
https://angelkey.com.au

*"I dedicate this book to St George and St Abu Sefin.
Both saints are renowned for their horse riding skills as much as their dedication to Christianity".*

I would like to acknowledge the Aboriginal and Torres Strait Islanders as the traditional custodians of the land.

I also extend my recognition to the Jagera and Meanjin Peoples, to whose lands I wrote this book on.

Finally, I pay my respects to the Jagera and Turrbal elders, past, present and emerging.

Alex was six years old when the people of Silver Town crowned her the "Horse princess".

Alex carried this unique title as a testament to her horseriding skills and talent.

Now nine years old, Alex knew she would forever be the "Horse Princess" of Silver Town.

Little did she know
that a new girl in Silver Town
would change that.

"Welcome Simone Mookee", announced Coach Verona gleefully.

Coach Verona took charge of training the best junior horse riders.

So, Alex now had some competition.

As soon as Coach Verona
finished her long speech,
Alex felt a pang of jealousy.

Alex began to think: 'Could Simone be better than me?'

But Alex would do anything to make Coach Verona proud.

So, Alex decided to welcome Simone to Silver Town.

Determined, Alex searched high and low for Simone.
But Simone was no where to be found.

Along the way to the classroom, Alex ran into Gigi crying.

"Gigi, what is wrong?", Alex asked with concern.

"Simone called me a fat and ugly duckling", Gigi cried.

Alex was speechless.

Gigi had never been bullied before.

While Alex comforted Gigi, she plotted revenge.

When the school bell rang, Alex made her way to talk with Mrs Bowman.

Mrs Bowman listened to Alex and gave her tips.

Tips on how to forgive.

Alex appreciated Mrs Bowman's listening ear and tips.

Gigi and Alex followed Mrs Bowman's advice.

Surprisingly, Simone and her family, left Silvertown the following week.

www.ingramcontent.com/pod-product-compliance
Lightning Source LLC
Chambersburg PA
CBHW042355070526
44585CB00028B/2939